Daffodils

Daffodils

A Wisley handbook

F. W. Shepherd

Cassell

The Royal Horticultural Society

Cassell Educational Limited
Artillery House
Artillery Row
London SW1P 1RT
for the Royal Horticultural Society

First published 1987
Second impression 1988

British Library Cataloguing in Publication Data

Shepherd, F. W.
    Daffodils. —(A Wisley handbook)
    1. Daffodils
    I. Title II. Royal Horticultural Society
    III. Series
    635.9′3425 SB413.D12
    ISBN 0-304-31129-4

Line drawings by Ian Foulis
Photographs by Michael Warren, the Harry Smith
Collection and Rosewarne Experimental Horticulture
Station

Design by Lynda Smith

Phototypesetting by Franklyn Graphics, Formby
Printed in Hong Kong by Wing King Tong Co. Ltd

Contents

Introduction

Thanks to the climate and to the skill of British growers, more daffodils are produced in this country than in any other. From the east coast of Scotland to Cornwall there are over 9,000 acres devoted to daffodils and it is estimated that about 50,000 tons of bulbs are handled each year—perhaps one thousand million bulbs to be lifted mechanically, dried, graded, stored and then replanted or sold.

Many are replanted for further reproduction and for the commercial production of cut flowers. (We usually say 'cutting' for market or for the house, but most of the outdoor flowers are actually picked by thrusting the thumb into the base of the flower stem and snapping it off as low as possible.) Some are used for forcing in greenhouses for early cut flowers, some are purchased for planting in public parks and some are exported.

However, several million bulbs are sold each year to ordinary gardeners, who buy them, usually in small quantities, for growing in pots indoors, for a spring display outside, after which they are removed, or for more permanent planting in beds, borders and grass. In most cases the bulbs survive to provide the first of the larger flowers of the season. And, although the snowdrop and crocus precede it as true harbingers of spring, it is the common yellow daffodil that tells us spring is really here.

This handbook sets out to assist the many people who buy daffodil bulbs to know more about them and to make the best use of them in the following years. It describes some of the thousands of cultivars available and explains their classification, and it advises on different planting situations. It also gives a brief introduction to the esoteric world of breeding and showing, together with a survey of pests and diseases.

Above: 'St Keverne', with its exceptionally rich yellow colouring, was raised in 1949 and is still grown commercially for cut flowers

Below left: 'Charity May', a Cyclamineus cultivar which regularly wins prizes at daffodil shows and is a good garden daffodil, increasing rapidly

Below right: 'Flower Record', one of the most popular bicolour large-cupped daffodils, dates from 1943

7

Daffodils in the wild

Daffodils belong to the genus *Narcissus*, one of several ornamental genera in the *Amaryllidaceae*, a family which is widespread throughout the world. Some, such as *Nerine*, *Galanthus* and *Hippeastrum* are useful decorative plants for the garden and greenhouse and are well known. Others, like *Pancratium* and *Hymenocallis*, with corona-like outgrowths to their flowers, are similar to *Narcissus* but more tender here and therefore less familiar.

In common usage the name daffodil is applied to the larger-flowered trumpet kinds with a single flower on each stem, while the name narcissi popularly refers to those with smaller flowers and sometimes more than one flower on each stem, usually derived from *N. poeticus*. It is, however, quite in order for all of them to be called daffodil or narcissus, as they will be in this book.

The original home of the narcissus is Spain and Portugal. There are now thought to be about 40 species, which in prehistoric times spread from there, each adapting to widely different habitats, and also multiplied to produce subspecies, varieties and forms. The species and its relatives known as the wild daffodil or Lent lily (*N. pseudonarcissus*) are distributed up the west coast of Europe to the north of England and over much of the rest of western Europe, many also remaining in Spain. This group includes those most generally known as daffodils. All tend to be found in areas of cold or cool winters with enough rain to result in moist soils, followed by warmer summers to dry the soil after flowering. They often occur in rather open woodland or meadow, where the flowers and leaves appear before light is excluded by the canopy of trees and tall grasses.

A slightly less hardy group, the Tazettas and their relatives (commonly known as "narcissi") are quite distinct in appearance. They too have dispersed in various directions, along both shores of the Mediterranean to Israel and its neighbours, with a few extending south down several hundred miles of the west coast of Africa and out into the Canary Islands. A related group is to be found much further east in Kashmir, China and Japan, although it is usually believed that man rather than any natural agency took them to those distant parts of the world. The bulbs of *N. tazetta* and most of its allies are beautifully round and encased in dark shining skins which, if kept dry, enable them to remain unharmed

Above: *Narcissus tazetta*, widely distributed throughout the Mediterranean and beyond, is the wild parent of the familiar "narcissi" which are so often grown as indoor bulbs for flowering at Christmas

Below: *Narcissus pseudonarcissus*, the wild daffodil or Lent lily as it is called, is a native of Britain but has become scarce in recent years

for months. Such attractive 'pre-packs', productive of striking scented flowers, would have been useful makeweight cargo in the camel trains trading between west and east in days gone by.

The various Tazettas and related Jonquils (N. *jonquilla* and its forms) are the exceptions to the rule that narcissus require cool winter temperatures if they are to thrive and flower on time. These more tender groups prefer the heat and drought of Mediterranean summers and the milder winter temperatures with ample water.

Some hardier species, the poet's narcissus (N. *poeticus*) and its relatives, have adapted themselves to the more spartan climates of the high mountains both north and south of the Mediterranean. There they flower a little later than others in lower altitudes and their progeny do the same in those gardens where they flourish. Often hidden in moist soil under snow in the winter, they emerge in spring and then continue in growth, since they rarely experience the extreme drought of the plains. These conditions promote a longer period of root growth, which also happens when they are transferred to gardens.

The remaining groups, N. *bulbocodium*, the hoop-petticoat, N. *cyclamineus* and N. *triandrus* hybrids and other small-flowered daffodils, have stayed closer to the Iberian peninsula. They mostly thrive in cool moist winter conditions, with a short or longer rest in the summer when leaves and roots die and the soil is dry.

NAMING AND CLASSIFICATION

Having been introduced into gardens at a very early stage in the history of man, daffodils have attracted much attention from botanists. The Greek Theophrastus listed and described many of the earliest known kinds in about 300 BC. However, by the seventeenth century the English herbalist Parkinson was already deploring the confusion over names of daffodils and since then, to make matters worse, a succession of botanists have studied, named and renamed the numerous variants found in the wild. At one period, during the early nineteenth century, *Narcissus* was split into 16 separate genera, named after mythical characters like Ajax and Ganymedes. These names might still be encountered occasionally, although only *Jonquilla* has survived in current usage. Modern botanists now recognize about 40 species and numerous sub-species within the one genus *Narcissus*.

The problem of nomenclature of the wild plants has been heightened by the fact that narcissus reproduce so easily in nature. Every slightly variable seedling produced may persist and increase itself by bulb division, to become a distinct variant which

'Paper White Grandiflora' bears pure white flowers, usually three to seven to a stem, and is ideal for pot culture in the home; it is rarely grown outside, except in the warmest parts of Britain

may deserve a new name. Such new plants found in the wild might be given a botanical or Latin name, for instance, *Narcissus tazetta* subsp. *lacticolor*. However, if the seedling occurs in cultivation, it will usually receive a cultivar name, such as *Narcissus* 'Scilly White'.

This scrupulous naming of distinct plants might seem irritating, but it is most important for both gardeners and commercial growers. To take a further example from *N. tazetta*, there are at least half a dozen named white-flowered kinds of this species, differing not only in the appearance of their flowers but in their growing habits and ability to survive in various conditions. These include *N. tazetta* subsp. *panizzianus*, *N. tazetta* subsp. *canariensis*, *N. tazetta* subsp. *pachybolbus*, *N.* 'Orientalis', *N.* 'Paper White' and *N.* 'Paper White Grandiflora' and *N.* 'Paper White Snowflake'. To purchase and plant any one of these white-flowered Tazettas in mistake for another could result in considerable disappointment and even loss to the buyer. Careful and accurate naming of wild and garden plants is therefore essential. (For the classification of garden daffodils, see p. 15).

Garden daffodils

HISTORY AND DEVELOPMENT

As we have seen, daffodils are among the oldest cultivated plants, particularly valued for their early flowers. New kinds were constantly being sought to add to the range and were either found and introduced from their native surroundings, or arose as chance seedlings or as the result of deliberate sowing of selected seed. However, it was only in the early nineteenth century that serious hybridizing began, ·with the work of William Herbert, Dean of Manchester. By wide crossing, he proved that many of the so-called species were in fact natural hybrids and, at the same time, showed something of the potential of the genus for producing different and attractive flowers. Herbert's example was soon followed by Edward Leeds, also in Lancashire, and by William Backhouse in County Durham. Leeds concentrated on hybridizing daffodils with white or pale flowers and as a result, these were given the name Leedsii in an early classification of garden daffodils by the botanist J. G. Baker of Kew. Baker also named other divisions after well-known breeders and growers of the period – Backhousei, Barrii, Burbidgei and Engleheartii.

In 1874 the nurseryman Peter Barr formed a group of enthusiasts to purchase the whole of Leeds's stock and later bought all Backhouse's bulbs. These acquisitions gave Barr's nursery the largest collection of daffodils of the day and the material on which Baker based his system of classification. Such was the interest in daffodils that in 1884 Barr published a booklet entitled *Ye Narcissus or Daffodil Flowere*. This coincided with the first edition of the *Little Booke of Daffodils* by the great Irish breeder, William Baylor Hartland of Cork, which continued to appear for nearly 30 years. In that same year, 1884, the first daffodil conference of the Royal Horticultural Society was held.

No doubt inspired by these events, other people took up daffodil breeding. They included the Reverend G. H. Engleheart who, for more than 50 years until his death in 1936, raised a large number of very diverse cultivars. Among them was 'Magnificence', for a time one of the most important early market yellow daffodils, but he is now generally remembered for the development of numerous forms of the poet's narcissus.

P. D. Williams of Lanarth in south Cornwall and his cousin, J. C.

'Carlton', an outstanding cultivar raised by the famous P. D. Williams in 1927, is still widely grown commercially for cutting and forcing

Williams (later of camellia and rhododendron fame), started breeding daffodils in the last decade of the nineteenth century. P. D. had considerable success with the Poetaz hybrids, between N. *poeticus* and N. *tazetta*, to which he generally gave Cornish place names. He registered his own 'Pride of Cornwall' in 1933, probably somewhat piqued that the van der Schoots of Hillegom had got in with 'Pride of Holland' for another Poetaz two years before. 'Carlton', a rather frilly yellow large cup, was also bred at Lanarth and now occupies many acres of bulb fields as one of the leading market daffodils.

Although the early breeding was predominantly English, the Dutch soon joined in. Others in the Celtic fringe apart from the Cornish were active too. The Brodie of Brodie of Forres in Scotland, then Guy Wilson of Broughshane in Northern Ireland and J. L. Richardson of Waterford in Ireland all added enormously to the range and quality of daffodil flowers. Many other people have produced new seedlings, named and un-named, most of which have disappeared within a few years, although some have persisted in commerce or in old gardens. It is difficult to spot a winner when it first flowers and even more difficult to explain why a few should be extant long after their introduction. 'Empress' and 'Emperor' were registered by the breeder William Backhouse in 1890 and 'Weardale Perfection' a few years later.

Acres of yellow trumpet daffodils are grown for bulbs and as cut flowers

The last, regarded as the greatest advance in trumpet daffodils, has almost disappeared, as has the bicolour 'Empress', but the all-yellow 'Emperor', lingers in many gardens and in hedges around bulb fields, although it has become very scarce in commerce. 'King Alfred', raised by another grower at about the same time, soon became the most important yellow trumpet for gardens and market and remained so until the 1950s when it was overtaken by 'Golden Harvest'; it is still available, but most stocks are now muddled with 'Rembrandt'. William Copeland, who was breeding daffodils at Southampton between the wars, produced some of the first successful doubles and these are still in cultivation. On the other hand, the different kinds raised and named by the Martins of Truro have all gone, except for 'Silver Chimes', that beautiful many-flowered white Tazetta (formerly classified as Triandrus) which is still popular. More recently the late Alec Gray, in the Isles of Scilly and then on mainland Cornwall, developed a range of delightful miniatures, including 'April Tears', 'Jumblie' and 'Tête-à-Tête'. These are not only being widely planted in gardens, but also used as parents.

Today daffodil breeding continues in many parts of the British Isles, as well as in the Netherlands, the USA, New Zealand and

14

Australia. There is now an enormous range of colours available, from pure white through shades of yellow to orange, pink and red, and in every conceivable combination and such a great variety of shapes that some are scarcely recognizable as daffodils.

CLASSIFICATION

The endless spate of new cultivars from the mid-nineteenth century onwards soon ran into thousands and it became necessary to classify or group them into divisions, for the benefit, particularly, of exhibitors and judges at the numerous shows and also as a guide for gardeners and commercial growers. The first daffodil conference arranged by the Royal Horticultural Society in 1884 made a start by abolishing the Latin names for the three main divisions and substituting English ones. Following further conferences and committees, a classified list of all known names was published by the RHS in 1907. A later list in 1916 gave 11 instead of 7 divisions and a total of more than 3,000 current names, plus some 600 that were 'lost or surpassed'.

Some of the divisions in these earlier classifications are no longer in use, although the names might still be encountered occasionally and should be explained. The Incomparabilis were strong-growing varieties most of which are now known as large cups. The Barrii, which later included the Burbidgei, a name rarely met with, were largely the present small-cupped cultivars. The Leedsii were all-white or near white flowers of any size which are now placed in the appropriate size division.

The Divisions

The current classification consists of 12 Divisions, which are summarized below. The classification is used in the catalogues of reputable nurserymen and should help gardeners when choosing and buying bulbs. It also serves as the basis for classes at flower shows. Note that corona is the botanical name for the central part of the narcissus flower; this is called a trumpet if it is roughly as long as or longer than the petals, and a cup or a corona if it is shorter. The petals, as they are familiarly known, are not true petals and should correctly be termed perianth segments.

Division 1: Trumpet daffodils of garden origin, with usually one flower on a stem and the trumpet as long or longer than the petals. Most of those we think of as real daffodils come here, although a few in the next Division look very similar.

Division 2: Large-Cupped or Long-Cupped daffodils of garden

'Cheerfulness' is representative of a double daffodil with two or three blooms on each stem and useful for its late flowering

origin, with one flower on a stem and the cup more than one third but less than equal to the length of the petals.

Division 3: Small-Cupped or Short-Cupped daffodils of garden origin, with usually one flower on a stem and the cup not more than one third the length of the petals. These require careful measurement to distinguish them from the previous Division and some also resemble those in Division 9. They mostly have the poet's narcissus in their parentage many generations back and tend to be all-white or bicoloured.

Division 4: Double daffodils of garden origin with fully double flowers or sometimes with a double corona only. Although not distinguished in the classification, there are two distinct types – those with only one, usually larger, bloom on each stem, derived mainly from the trumpet and cup daffodils; and those with two or more blooms on each stem, derived from the Poetaz and other smaller-flowered kinds.

Division 5: Triandrus daffodils of garden origin, usually with two or three blooms on each stem. They are normally about 6 inches (15 cm) high, sometimes taller, and the flowers may be nodding, with the corona somewhat rounded and about as broad as it is long. The petals are often swept back, but not so obviously as in *N. cyclamineus*.

Division 6: Cyclamineus daffodils of garden origin. The species, *N. cyclamineus*, occurs wild in Portugal and is slightly similar to its neighbour *N. triandrus* in appearance, with nodding flowers and swept-back petals. However, it differs in rarely having more than one flower on each stem and markedly in the longer narrow corona. It bears some resemblance to a cyclamen – whence the name. The garden daffodils derived from it have rather shorter cups and broader petals.

Division 7: Jonquilla daffodils of garden origin. Most of the Jonquils or rush-leaved narcissus have the characteristic jonquil scent, some more than others, and usually two or three flowers on each stem. The leaves are dark green instead of the normal grey-green of other daffodils and sometimes more or less rolled rather than flat.

Division 8: Tazetta daffodils of garden origin. As we have seen, the species, *N. tazetta*, and its relations are less hardy than most daffodils. Also known as polyanthus or bunch-flowered narcissus, those which are obviously derived from *N. tazetta* have many flowers on each stem, sometimes up to 20 or more, with rounded or goblet-shaped cups and mostly a powerful and distinctive scent. The leaves and stems are dark green as in the Jonquils.

Extensive breeding between Tazettas and Poeticus daffodils (of the next Division) has produced a group of cultivars known as Poetaz. These are not separately classified but placed here and have a few flowers on each stem, which are larger than most other Tazetta cultivars, usually scented and with a brightly coloured shallow corona and white or pale yellow petals.

Division 9: Poeticus daffodils of garden origin. Like the species, *N. poeticus*, and its wild forms, they have white petals and flat flared cups, of bright red or with a red rim. They can be very difficult to distinguish from Division 3, but the difference is often in the parentage, since they are derived from *N. poeticus* alone. The white of the petals also tends to have a pure sparkling quality and they have their own perfume, not quite so cloying as in the Tazettas and Jonquils.

Division 10: All *Narcissus* species and their wild forms, varieties and natural hybrids. Technically, therefore, this Division includes *N. triandrus*, *N. cyclamineus*, *N. jonquilla*, *N. tazetta* and *N. poeticus*, although the garden hybrids derived from them belong

Above: 'Jenny', a neat Cyclamineus daffodil with the distinctive swept back petals and nodding flowers, was awarded a First Class Certificate in 1950

Below: 'Sundial', a dainty Jonquil with the dark green leaves characteristic of the Division

to earlier Divisions and the species themselves are often wrongly grouped with them. Others in general cultivation are *N. bulbocodium*, the hoop-petticoat, and its forms; *N. pseudonarcissus*, the native daffodil, and its numerous sub-species; *N. × biflorus*; and the dwarf *N. asturiensis* and *N. minor*.

Division 11: Split-Corona daffodils, with the corona split for at least one third of its length (under the current definition). Sometimes called collar, butterfly or orchid-flowered daffodils, these interesting cultivars are the most recent addition to the Divisions and were first included in the 1969 edition of the *International Register*. They are the result of a breeding programme by a Dutch bulb company, begun more than 50 years ago, and attracted much unfavourable comment at first. They are certainly different from the established idea of a daffodil with the split corona and often very frilled rim.

Division 12: Miscellaneous daffodils not falling into any of the other Divisions. This Division is simply to allow for any new and unclassifiable daffodil that might turn up. At present it contains very few cultivars, mostly derived from *N. bulbocodium*.

The colour code

Until 1975 the first three Divisions were subdivided according to the colour combinations of perianth and corona. However, following suggestions from the American Daffodil Society, a more accurate colour code has been introduced, in which capital initial letters are used after the number of each Division to indicate the colours of different parts of the flower:
    These abbreviations are:

W	white or whitish	P	pink
G	green	O	orange
Y	yellow	R	red

The letters are always arranged in the same order. The first one or two letters refer to the colour of the perianth (or petals); and the next one or three letters describe the colour(s) of the corona (trumpet or cup), subdivided into the inner or eye zone, the middle zone and the outer zone or rim; in the case of doubles, two letters may be used for the corona if appropriate.
    Thus an all-yellow trumpet is 1Y–Y and a bicolour trumpet is 1W–Y; 2Y–YYR is a large-cupped cultivar with yellow petals and yellow cup with a red rim.

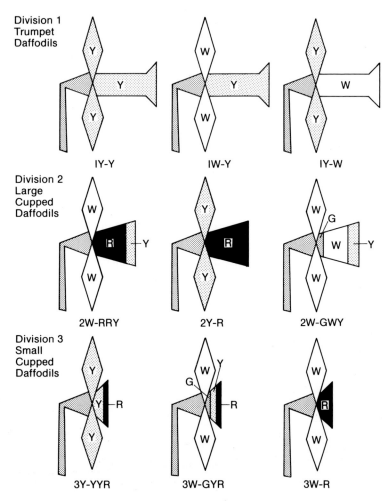

Division 1
Trumpet
Daffodils

1Y-Y   1W-Y   1Y-W

Division 2
Large
Cupped
Daffodils

2W-RRY   2Y-R   2W-GWY

Division 3
Small
Cupped
Daffodils

3Y-YYR   3W-GYR   3W-R

Y = yellow
W = white
R = red
G = green (normally only visible from the face view and not in profile)

Examples of the colour code

NATIONAL COLLECTION

The main national collection of *Narcissus*, which contains ov
1,000 cultivars of worldwide origin, is held by the University
Ulster, Coleraine, Northern Ireland. It serves as a reference f
identification, shows how the genus has developed and is
valua

The daffodil plant

A brief description of the typical daffodil plant may be helpful to the gardener.

Basically, the only permanent stem of any daffodil, and of many other bulbs, is the flat or slightly conical disc found at the base of the bulb when it is cut vertically in half. From this stem the new roots grow downwards in a circle around the edge of the bulb. Once started, as soon as the bulb receives sufficient moisture in late summer or autumn, the roots grow quite rapidly and, if the soil is deep and open, to a considerable depth (3 ft [90 cm] and more has been recorded). As with all other plants, the roots hold the whole plant in position and also absorb water and the plant food dissolved in it, together with any harmful substances such as herbicides present in the soil. Without roots, many bulbs left out of the ground will struggle to produce leaves, and flowers if they are present, at the usual time, but there will then be little or no new growth of the bulb or flowers in the following year.

The roots persist until the following spring or early summer, when the leaves die down and the roots too die away, leaving the bulb rootless and leafless until growth recommences in the late summer or early autumn. Different kinds of daffodil vary a little in their root and leaf growth. Some roots start when the bulb

Tazettas are still widely grown in the Isles of Scilly for the cut flower market.

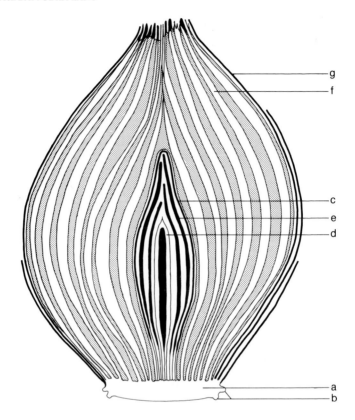

Structure of a narcissus bulb

(a) Basal stem	(b) Embryo roots	(c) Flower bud	(d) Embryo flower bud
(e) Embryo foliage leaves	(f) Fleshy scale leaves	(g) Outer scale leaves

becomes only slightly moist and continue long into the following summer, sometimes remaining while new roots begin to grow. This tendency is particularly apparent in cultivars derived from the poet's narcissus. Others take longer to root in the autumn and lose their roots more promptly in the spring, especially when the weather is dry. This is noticeable in the Tazetta group.

Whatever the pattern of root growth, the sooner rooting recommences in late summer the sooner the plant begins to function in the ground and the better growth will be in the spring. Early planting is therefore to be recommended, for it not only ensures early rooting, unless the soil is extremely dry, but prevents moisture in the air causing premature rooting and consequent damage to the roots during planting.

Returning to the primitive stem or disc at the base of the bulb, it is from here that the leaves grow upwards and out of the top with a number of scales between them. The leaves become green as they emerge into the light, while the scales remain below ground or only slightly above the surface. The green leaves last through spring and early summer, converting the simple chemicals absorbed by the roots into materials for the development of all parts of the plant. Once they have served their purpose – which in nature may be when they are denied the necessary light by over-head growth of other plants or are smothered by them, or when water is no longer available for the roots to function – they die away. The flower stem dies with the leaves and, at the same time, the base of the leaves and the scales swell to create the new bulb or bulbs that develop within the old. The old outer scales are pushed outwards to form the dry protective scales found on all daffodil bulbs.

The flower bud on its stalk or stem is formed in the centre of the cluster of leaves when the bulb is sufficiently large and mature. Very large bulbs may also produce a second flower from among another cluster of leaves within the bulb, but only if the original bulb has developed two instead of one cluster of leaves in the previous season, which leads to the formation of a new bulb at the end of the season. It is more usual for such new bulbs to become almost or quite detached from the old bulb before a flower is produced. A daffodil bulb that is growing well will normally have a central cluster of three or more leaves enclosing a flower bud on its stalk, a second group of usually two leaves, and an outer cluster of leaves on a bulblet which is becoming detached from its parent

The Cyclamineus cultivar, 'Jack Snipe', is suitable for naturalizing in grass or growing in a rockery or peat garden

and which may or may not contain a flower bud. The flower bud is produced in the bulb as and after the leaves die down and is fully developed in every detail before the end of the summer and before new roots appear.

The cycle of growth is affected not only by the presence or absence of water but also by temperature. The rate of growth of leaves and flowers is increased by higher temperatures and slowed down by lower ones. However, the leaves and flower stems will continue to grow at quite low temperatures once started, as may be observed when daffodils appear in late winter and then become covered with a blanket of snow. The temperature of the soil is kept just above freezing, which enables the leaves to continue in growth even when frozen conditions prevail above ground.

The majority of daffodils, except the Tazettas, need a spell of cool temperatures before the stem of the fully developed flower starts to elongate. Careful research has shown that the critical figure is 48°F (9°C) and that the longer bulbs are stored at or below this temperature the more rapid subsequent growth will be. This temperature is one that can be expected in the soil in the open in Britain and in other countries where cool or cold winters are experienced.

Such knowledge of the effect of temperature on the rate of growth has been used to develop a system in which bulbs are stored at different temperatures after lifting and before replanting in order to produce earlier or later flowers. Bulbs treated in this way are lifted early, just before the leaves die down, and stored for a very short time at high temperatures to ensure that formation of the flower buds for the next season is complete. The regimes vary according to the time of flowering required. For the earliest flowers, bulbs are stored at up to 86°F (30°C) for a week or two, followed by steady drops to 68°F (20°C) and 63°F (17°C), before cool storing at 48°F (9°C) commences. Flowers that reach the market well before Christmas each year are often produced by this method from bulbs forced in greenhouses, although there are also those from the Isles of Scilly which naturally bloom early.

Bulbs treated in such a way are described as prepared and can be purchased by gardeners for growing indoors, in bowls and pots, or outside in the garden. It is important to remember that all this careful preparation can be nullified if the bulbs are subject to higher temperatures in transit or left in warm surroundings after arrival. When planting them in the open, the soil should be well watered to cool it and the bulbs deeply buried to protect them from the heat of the sun. (See p. 36 for forced indoor bulbs.)

Choosing and buying bulbs

Millions of bulbs are sold each year through various outlets – general stores, garden centres, nurseries, roadside stalls and by mail order through the weekend and gardening press.

Mixed bulbs offer a reasonable selection at a low price and can be a good choice for the gardener who is growing daffodils for the first time. Controlled mixtures made up with proportionate amounts of specific cultivars are available from at least one major British firm. These are very popular with the public, as are collections of bulbs designed for pots and bowls, flower arranging and so on. Unfortunately, however, some mixtures are more of a lottery. They may consist of rogue bulbs left behind in the ground after the first lifting of individual named cultivars, which have lost their labels and are easier to lift *en masse* and sell as mixed; or they may simply be an assortment of outdoor cut-flower bulbs.

Many of the named cultivars offered in garden centres are Dutch cut-flower bulbs imported and distributed wholesale by firms based in Lincolnshire. Some are also grown for wholesale purposes in this country. Because of the huge quantities required, these tend to be older cultivars like 'King Alfred', 'Magnificence' and 'Unsurpassable' and are predominantly trumpets and large cups in bright colours. More recently, however, the range of wholesale bulbs has been expanded to include miniatures and split-corona daffodils which, being less suitable cut flowers for the market, are usually more expensive.

Undoubtedly the finest choice is provided by specialist bulb nurserymen and daffodil growers, who advertise in newspapers and gardening journals for postal purchase or exhibit at spring shows where orders may be taken. (For a list of suppliers, see p. 64).

Daffodil bulbs are usually lifted in June and July and then dried, cleaned, graded and prepared for sale from mid-August onwards. Sales continue through the late summer and many mail order nurseries do not deliver until later September or early October, although early ordering and delivery are preferable. Bulbs should be planted as soon as possible on arrival and for the best results should be in the ground by mid-September.

In the trade and among daffodil enthusiasts, several technical terms are used to describe the different sizes and shapes of bulbs. It is helpful to know them, although unlikely that the gardener will actually have to ask for bulbs by these names.

Mother bulbs have two or three new bulbs or offsets still attached at the base. They can be expected to produce one or two flower stems in the first year after planting and will increase considerably as the offsets become detached and ready for flowering.

Offsets are new bulbs which have developed to the stage of breaking away from the mother bulb, either naturally or artificially by means of a gentle tug if they are loose enough. They usually produce one set of two or three leaves in the first year, but rarely flower stems until the following year when they have grown to a good size.

Chips are very small offsets. (The term is also applied to segments of a daffodil bulb. See p. 55.)

Types of bulb

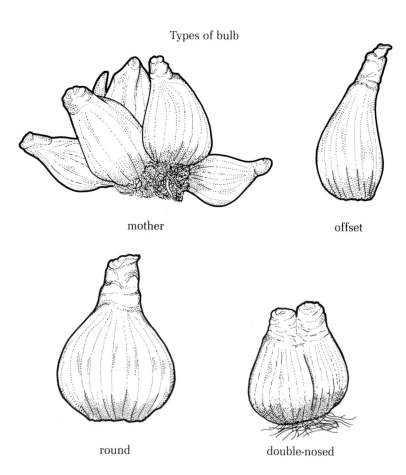

mother

offset

round

double-nosed

Rounds are bulbs with a single growing point or nose visible at the top. They will normally produce only one set of leaves and one flower stem, although very small rounds may not flower at all in the first year.

Double-nosed bulbs consist of a round and a large offset still closely attached and therefore have two distinct growing points. From each of these a set of leaves will appear and often a flower stem among the leaves. Good double-nosed bulbs producing two flowers will give the best display in pots and beds, although those with only one flower will have rather more leaves than flowers.

As lifted means that the sample will contain a miscellany of bulbs of all sizes, shapes and ages which have been lifted one, two or more years after planting and not graded.

Drifts of naturalized daffodils in the famous garden at Sissinghurst Castle, Kent; most have been growing there for many years and the names have been lost

Where and how to grow daffodils

A place can be found for daffodils in every type and size of garden and in almost every situation from formal beds and borders to open grass, as well as in the house and greenhouse. Out of doors, daffodils grow best in open situations, although they will stand some shade. They succeed in almost any well-drained soil with ample water in spring and early summer. However, very acid peaty soils are not satisfactory, while in very light quick-draining soils in districts with low rainfall they tend to produce smaller bulbs and flowers.

Regular feeding is rarely necessary. As with all plants, of course, nitrogen induces taller leaves with a richer colour, phosphates encourage root growth and potash gives colour to flowers and sturdier leaf growth. Nevertheless, experiments and experience have shown little evidence that daffodils benefit from the application of these main plants foods as a fertilizer. It is more important, in thin soils, to incorporate plenty of decayed organic matter to improve moisture retention.

In the case of extremely poor soil lacking in nutrients, a complete fertilizer can be applied at the time of planting or soon after the appearance of the leaves. The ever-popular Growmore or a similar product which does not contain too much nitrogen would be suitable, at a rate of 4 oz per square yard (135 g per m²). It should be borne in mind that the roots begin to absorb plant food with the soil water from the time that they emerge from the bulb in autumn. If fertilizer is applied too late, it may never reach the growing tips of the roots underground unless rainfall is very heavy.

Double daffodils, in particular N. *poeticus* 'Flore Pleno', may also benefit from feeding and watering in dry spells in early spring, to prevent withering of the flower buds. (See also p. 37 for feeding indoors.)

Failure to flower is one of the gardener's commonest complaints about daffodils and, although this may be caused by eelworm or large narcissus fly, or perhaps by a virus (see p. 61), the most usual reason is overcrowding of the bulbs, with consequent lack of room, water and nutrients. As we have seen, a single bulb develops one or more new ones each season. After about ten years or more, the clumps of bulbs become so congested that they have little chance of reaching flowering size and can only produce a mass of leaves. The solution is to lift and divide the clusters of bulbs as the leaves are dying down, usually in July, and replant them individually. A complete fertilizer may also be dug in at the time of replanting to improve vigour. All should then flower after a couple of years in their new homes.

IN GRASS

Many daffodils look best when growing naturally in rough grass or a meadow area of fine grass, in an orchard beneath fruit trees or in woodland. The kinds of daffodil to choose and the number to plant will obviously depend on the amount of room available and the character of the grass and other vegetation already growing there. However, it must be stressed that this method is only successful when the bulbs are planted in great quantity, by the hundred at least; it is no good having five of each cultivar. Large pieces of ground can safely accommodate the biggest modern cultivars, which would seem overbearing in a more restricted space. Even so, the smaller daffodils can be just as effective as the giants of today if planted sufficiently densely and often seem more appropriate in such a setting. It is also worth remembering that daffodils may grow taller than usual and become ungainly in the shade of trees and that dwarf ones are often preferable for this reason. The only problem is that they may be choked if the grass mixture is too coarse. The Cyclamineus cultivars from Division 6 are particularly suitable for naturalizing, together with smaller species such as the wild English daffodil, N. pseudonarcissus. For short grass, N. asturiensis, N. bulbocodium and its relatives and N. triandrus albus (correctly N. triandrus triandrus) can be recommended.

Daffodils grown in grass are probably most attractive in groups or drifts devoted to the same species or cultivar (perhaps over-lapping at the edges), as can be seen in the alpine garden at Wisley with its mass of N. bulbocodium. Some firms offer mixtures designed for naturalizing. Otherwise, one can plant cheap ready-mixed bulbs or make up one's own mixture.

So, as with all gardening, decide on the planting scheme required and plan accordingly. Having estimated the area to be covered, allow up to half a dozen bulbs per square foot (0.09 m^2), which will produce a colourful display in the first season and a continuing show in subsequent years as the bulbs fill the space. Closer planting will, of course, achieve an immediate massed effect, but may not give room for future growth of the bulbs. For the most natural and attractive results, they should be distributed unevenly, not in rows or uniformly spaced. With small quantities, a good method is to scatter the bulbs at the intended rate and plant where they fall. On a large scale, it is often easier to lift a square of turf about 18 inches (45 cm) across, with a spade, and plant in a cluster, then replace and firm in the square.

Planting directly into grass is not the easiest of gardening operations, particularly when carried out at the right time of year, often after a dry summer or before the autumn rains have softened the surface of the ground. Tools are also a problem: an ordinary garden trowel, a short single-handed bulb planter or an old-fashioned wooden dibber are not really adequate in dense grass or hard ground, while a spade is too large for the purpose. The best type of bulb planter has a long handle of about 3 feet (0.9 m), with a crosspiece so that it can be driven into the ground with the foot, and may be bought from specialist suppliers or made up by a local blacksmith. An alternative is a crowbar, which can be moved around in the soil to widen the hole according to the size of the bulb.

In general the depth of the hole should be three times that of the height of the bulb. In other words, a 2-inch (5 cm) high bulb requires a hole 6 inches (15 cm) deep. In heavy clay soils, however, the hole should be only twice the size of the bulb. After planting the bulb, it is a good idea to break up the soil before filling in the hole, which will promote growth of the leaves in their first year. If using a crowbar, which forms a pointed hole, make it a little deeper and drop some fine soil into the bottom first to provide a base for the bulb at the correct depth and encourage early rooting. The bulbs will need little further attention. The grass should have been cut low, although not necessarily lawn-like, before planting and is unlikely to grow much more in late summer and early autumn. The daffodil leaves will begin to emerge from early spring onwards, according to climate and cultivar, and therefore working and walking over the ground should be avoided. The grass will start to grow at about the same time, but the daffodils should keep pace and show their flowers well.

After flowering, the developing seed pods may be picked off, except with those kinds such as N. *bulbocodium* that increase themselves by seeding rather than division. The removal of the pod slightly improves the growth of the bulb and the number of flowers in the following year, by enabling the plant to concentrate on feeding the bulb in the absence of seed. In most cases, self-sown seedlings are not desirable because they will differ from the parents and introduce unwanted variation in the overall scheme. They will also give rise to too many plants and these will become overcrowded and weak – a problem which anyway besets daffodils in grass.

Above: a sea of daffodils growing in woodland at Hodnet Hall in Shropshire

Below: a bed of Narcissus 'Trousseau', a beautiful bicolour trumpet, beneath a fine specimen of Magnolia x loebneri 'Leonard Messel'

Bulbs that are well spaced at planting will flower and multiply happily for many years. However, they will eventually become overcrowded and produce fewer flowers unless lifted and replanted at a wider spacing (see p. 28).

Grass cutting should not commence until the leaves die down in late June and July. However, if it is intended that the bulbs should seed themselves, mowing must be delayed until the seeds have dropped. They will then grow into new bulbs and flower in about five years. Alternatively, the grass can be cut earlier while the daffodil leaves are still green, but if this is done regularly, it will gradually weaken the bulbs and may destroy them completely. This was confirmed in a ten-year trial at the RHS Garden, Wisley, when bulbs from which the foliage was cut two weeks after flowering soon ceased flowering and most were killed. Those whose leaves were cut four weeks after flowering were severely weakened. Cutting after six weeks, but before the leaves were dead, produced leaf and flower growth almost equal to that of uncut control plants. Grass cuttings should be cleared away after the first and second cuts, although later short trimmings can be left. A relatively smooth surface is a better background for spring flowers and too much dead grass in the winter may encourage mice to nest and become a nuisance, if no more.

IN LAWNS

Early bulbs such as snowdrops and crocuses can be planted in fine grass and do not suffer too much if mown over soon after flowering in the interests of the lawn. Many of the miniature daffodils can also be treated in this way, although the early mowing immediately after flowering will soon reduce the bulbs to non-flowering size. This form of daffodil growing is expensive and not very practical, for the bulbs must be regarded as biennial or even annual and will need replacing every year or so.

IN ROCK GARDENS

Little groups of miniature daffodils may be planted in pockets of soil among low-growing alpines in a rock garden, where they will give a delightful display in spring and should continue to thrive for many years. Their leaves are mostly unobtrusive and they are small enough not to overshadow their neighbours. Three to five bulbs of the same kind, planted 3 to 5 inches (8–13 cm) apart (or less, depending on how miniature they are) and at the depth already recommended (p. 30), will generally fit in well without being too dominant. In larger rock gardens, bulbs can be massed in drifts, perhaps spilling over into an adjoining alpine meadow. The dead leaves should be removed after they have died in the summer, but otherwise they will require little attention.

Miniatures like N. *cyclamineus*, N. *bulbocodium* and its relatives N. *bulbocodium citrinus*, N. *obesus* and N. *romieuxii*, together with Cyclamineus cultivars such as 'Jenny', 'Jack Snipe', 'Tête-à-Tête', 'Little Witch' and 'Peeping Tom', are all particularly recommended for a rock garden. So too are the species N. *asturiensis* and N. *minor*, which are small relatives of the trumpet daffodils, and the several cultivars derived from N. *jonquilla*, like 'Lintie' and 'Sundial'. Other suitable garden varieties are the small trumpets from Division 1 such as 'W. P. Milner', 'Little Beauty', 'Little Gem', and 'Small Talk'; the small cups from Division 2, for instance 'Picoblanco', 'Xit' and 'Segovia'; the dwarf Triandrus from Division 5 like 'April Tears', 'Arctic Morn' and 'Hawera'; and the quaint double 'Rip van Winkle'.

AMONG SHRUBS AND IN MIXED BORDERS

The large-flowered modern trumpets and large cups are especially suitable for growing under shrubs and in borders. They may be arranged in circular clumps of a dozen or so each between the shrubs, or planted around the base of shrubs that tend to become leggy or are being grown as standards. Where the border has been designed to present a solid mass of foliage and flowers (an admirable objective in my view), the bulbs will eventually be smothered and flower no longer. But they will have served their purpose of providing colour for a few years while the shrubs are developing.

In a formal shrubbery with strictly pruned individual specimens, daffodils can be planted in quantity to give an early display before many of the shrubs come into flower.

It should be remembered that larger daffodils produce at least 18 inches (45 cm) of foliage at or after flowering, which will fall and die away as the season advances. At this stage not only do the leaves look unsightly, but they may stifle smaller plants or damage the verge of the lawn. To avoid this, plant the daffodils at least 18 inches (45 cm) back from the edge of the border and place smaller earlier-flowering bulbs in front of them, such as crocuses, grape hyacinths and scillas, whose foliage will not be unduly harmed by the larger daffodil leaves.

IN HERBACEOUS BORDERS

Daffodils may be planted in groups between herbaceous plants, in the same way as among shrubs. However, they may need slightly deeper planting to prevent them being disturbed or lost during the annual autumn forking over which is necessary to keep a herbaceous border in trim.

Another way round this difficulty is to bury a few bulbs beneath herbaceous plants, particularly later-flowering ones, when these are being divided and replanted. The daffodil flowers and leaves will emerge through the young herbaceous shoots before there is much else to be seen in the border and, as the summer progresses, their dying leaves will be hidden by the taller growth of the herbaceous plants. Daffodils can survive for several years in such positions, as the leaves get enough light to mature and provide food for the bulb, although this method will only work with herbaceous plants that do not have dense roots.

AS BEDDING PLANTS

Some gardeners still like to devote part of their gardens to spring and summer bedding and, despite the considerable labour involved in planning, planting and weeding, can achieve two or even three striking shows of colour each year. The traditional bedding plants are mostly annuals and biennials, together with bulbs such as tulips and hyacinths. Large bold daffodils can also be effective, on their own or mingled with other plants.

The simplest method of using daffodils for bedding is to plant good sized round or double-nosed bulbs in staggered rows 4 to 6 inches (10–15 cm) apart each way. They need not be so deeply planted as in grass, only about twice their depth, which also makes them easier to lift. The time of planting will depend on when the summer bedding is removed, but is not too important since the bulbs will in any case be lifted and replanted elsewhere after flowering to make way for later bedding plants.

Rather than confining the display to one kind of daffodil, which will give a relatively brief burst of bloom, an early- and a late-flowering cultivar can be planted – for example, 'Golden Harvest' followed by 'Actaea', or 'Magnificence' by 'Cheerfulness'. However, this will mean deadheading the earlier ones as they fade, if they are not to spoil the effect of the later ones. Prepared bulbs can also be used for a very early show.

The taller daffodils associate well with shorter-growing forget-me-nots, polyanthus and wallflowers, providing a splash of bright yellow or white to relieve the various blues and reds. The bulbs are planted, with a trowel, between the biennials and at the same time as them, after removing summer bedding and preparing the soil. The bulbs and biennials in turn are cleared after flowering to

Daffodils make an effective contribution to a mixed spring border at Sissinghurst Castle

make room for the summer bedding. Bulbs lifted prematurely in this way, before the leaves have made their full growth, will not flower well the following season. However, they are certainly worth saving for future years and may be planted permanently among shrubs or naturalized in grass, or else left temporarily in the vegetable garden to recover before being lifted again two years later and replanted elsewhere.

Almost any of the cheaper cultivars can be used for bedding, although the shorter-stemmed kinds are probably better for planting on their own. Among the obvious favourites are 'Golden Harvest', 'Carlton' and 'Fortune', which require a fairly sheltered spot as the stems snap quite easily, 'La Riante' and 'White Lion'.

IN WINDOW BOXES AND OUTDOOR CONTAINERS

Daffodils are ideal for growing in window boxes or pots outside, to adorn a patio or paved area around the house. The bulbs may be planted at the usual time, either direct into the container, or alternatively in pots, which are then plunged in the container when they are about to flower. They are probably best removed after flowering, because of the mass of untidy foliage left, and treated in the same way as bulbs used for bedding.

The shorter-growing daffodils, about 12 inches (30 cm) high or less, are generally most appropriate for containers. There is a wide selection, particularly among the Cyclamineus cultivars in

Division 6, which include 'Charity May', 'Dove Wings', 'February Gold', 'Jenny', 'Larkelly', 'Little Witch' and 'Trewirgie' and the slightly taller 'Garden Princess'. The Triandrus daffodils of Division 5, like 'Rippling Waters', 'Thoughtful' and 'Tresamble', from 12 to 16 inches (30–40 cm) high, are also excellent, together with the Jonquils from Division 7, such as 'Buttercup', 'Sweetness' and 'Trevithian' which are slightly taller.

IN THE HOME AND GREENHOUSE

The forcing of daffodils in home or greenhouse further extends their usefulness and flowering period. Bowls of daffodils indoors give much pleasure from just before Christmas onwards, while some of the smallest species and cultivars can only be properly appreciated when they are growing in pots in a greenhouse.

For early indoor flowering, prepared bulbs should be bought (see p. 24), potted as soon as possible, in late August or early September, and then left in a cool place until ready for moving inside. A position in deep shade on the north side of a wall, covered with a 6-inch (15 cm) layer of ashes or peat, is best. The bulbs may be grown either in pots with drainage holes, or in bowls without. No fertilizers are required in either case. The pots, usually 6 to 9 inches (15–22 cm) in diameter, should be filled with a loam-based compost of the John Innes type and will, of course need saucers underneath when brought into the home. Bowls, on the other hand, are better filled with a peat-based compost, peat or proprietory bulb fibre and they can later be cleaned to stand direct on windowsills or furniture. However, the bulbs will not be in such good condition at the end of the season as those grown in pots and certainly not suitable for further forcing.

For a more spectacular display, bulbs may be planted in two layers, using round or tight double-nosed kinds if possible. The first three bulbs are placed deep in the pot or bowl on a layer of compost and more compost added between them, not quite covering the tips. Four more bulbs are then positioned in the gaps, one in the middle and three around the sides, and the container is topped up with compost to within an inch or so of the rim. The leaves of all seven bulbs should emerge almost together and they will all flower at the same time. If using smaller bulbs, larger numbers can be planted in each layer.

The bulbs should soon be filling the containers with roots and by mid-November there should be some sign of the leaves beginning to emerge. The containers can then be moved to a cool greenhouse or unheated room and, once the leaves have become completely green and the flower buds are visible, to a heated

'Dove Wings', like many other Cyclamineus cultivars, is ideal in size and scale for a window box or outside container; it is also a leading show daffodil

greenhouse or warm windowsill indoors. At this stage it is very important that they are kept moist and it may be beneficial to feed them with a liquid fertilizer such as Tomorite when watering. Some of the taller kinds will need support. A single stick in the centre or three around the edge at the expected height of the leaves and a light tie with raffia or soft green string should keep the leaves and flowers from flopping over.

Almost all the common daffodils can be grown for early indoor flowering in this way, but many of the tallest are not very elegant when clustered together and become even lankier as a result of forcing. The popular favourites are the Tazettas, particularly 'Paper White', 'Grand Soleil d'Or' and 'Cragford'. The much shorter 'Minnow' and 'Canaliculatus' also do well indoors. The Tazettas and their derivatives adapt better to growing in bowls than other narcissus and do not require cooling after potting. They should not be subjected to high temperatures before the leaves appear, but they will make good roots once planted in moist compost or fibre and will develop their leaves quite quickly.

Untreated bulbs can also be grown successfully in pots and bowls in the home to flower at the normal time. They should be kept in a fairly cool place until just before flowering.

An indoor trial of pot-grown daffodils was held at Wisley in 1986 and, out of the 36 entries, six received the Award of Merit and four were Highly Commended. The bulbs were planted in 6-inch (15 cm) pots, in two layers of three, using John Innes

Daffodils growing in pots in an alpine house make a lovely display

potting compost no. 2, from mid-October to mid-November. The pots were then plunged into sand in a cold frame and brought into a cold greenhouse in early February, where they flowered from mid-March into April. The award-winning plants, all 18 to 20 inches (45–50 cm) tall, were two trumpets, 'Glacier' 1W–W and 'Golden Rapture' 1Y–Y; a large cup, 'Romance' 2W–P; two doubles, 'Manly' 4Y—O and 'Petit Four' 4Y–P; and a Jonquil, 'Sugarbush' 7W–YYW.

The miniatures already mentioned in connection with the rock garden (see p.33) are ideal in an alpine house or cold greenhouse. Protected from wind and frost and from slugs and other pests, they can be seen more easily and at a more convenient height than when growing outside in the ground. They should be potted in good compost from August onwards and are best stood in a cool place until November, when they can be brought into the greenhouse to flower. A little feeding with liquid fertilizer after flowering will improve the bulbs for the following year and, as the leaves die down, the pots may be dried off for a few weeks before returning them to cooler conditions for the autumn. They should be shaken out of their pots when the leaves are completely dead and the bulbs repotted immediately.

Recommended daffodils

With the wide range of cultivars available today and the use of modern treatments, daffodils can be in flower from Christmas to May, and even from October in the milder counties. As a broad generalization, the first to flower are the Tazettas, when grown outside in warmer gardens, and the last are the doubles and Poets. 'Autumn Sol' blooms more or less regularly out of doors in October in Cornwall, while N. poeticus recurvus, the pheasant's eye, and N. poeticus 'Flore Pleno', the double white, are among the latest to bloom in May, the double usually surviving into June. 'Frigid', a small cup, also flowers in May and sometimes lasts into June.

The following lists include some of the most popular and reliable cultivars in each Division, which are easily obtainable from nurserymen and many garden centres. A few slightly more expensive kinds, unusual cultivars and recent introductions are also mentioned, all stocked by at least one specialist grower. (For an explanation of the colour code, see p. 19; and see also the previous chapter for recommendations for particular situations.)

DIVISION 1: TRUMPET DAFFODILS

Well known all-yellow cultivars (Y–Y) are 'Dutch Master', with a strong sturdy stem and bold flowers; 'Golden Harvest', which is shorter; and 'Unsurpassable', probably the largest although not the most shapely. 'King Alfred', the standard yellow in the past, is an interesting comparison with modern trumpets but no longer widely available as an individual cultivar. 'Kingscourt' has been a show quality flower for many years.

Among the bicolours (W–Y) are 'Foresight', which is fairly early; the aptly named 'Queen of Bicolors'; 'Prologue', another valuable early daffodil; 'Trousseau', one of the better paler ones (see p. 31); and the old 'Newcastle', with large well formed flowers.

Some of the most popular white trumpets (W–W) are 'Broughshane', 'Mount Hood' and 'Silent Valley', although they lack the purity of some others. 'Beersheba' is more graceful and 'Cantatrice', a long-established flower of good shape, is still worth a place in gardens. 'April Love' is a magnificent exhibition cultivar and an excellent garden plant.

39

An unusually attractive reverse bicolour (Y–W) is 'Spellbinder', while 'Honeybird' is a more recent example.

One of the first of the pink trumpets (W–P) was 'Mrs R. O. Backhouse', now being superseded by much more expensive cultivars.

Less common trumpets worth seeking out include 'Rijnveld's Early Sensation' Y–Y, which flowers as early as January outside; 'W. P. Milner' W–W, a dwarf daffodil suitable for the rock garden or cold greenhouse; and two newcomers, 'Bob Minor' Y–Y and 'Small Fry' Y–Y, which are useful in pots and at the front of a border outdoors for their short stems and leaves. One of the few orange trumpets (Y–O) is 'Brer Fox'.

DIVISION 2: LARGE-CUPPED DAFFODILS

Some of these cultivars have cups nearly as long as the petals and are almost indistinguishable from the trumpets. They include many of the pink daffodils (W–P), such as 'Debutante' and 'Passionale'.

Of the all-yellows (Y–Y), the richly coloured 'Galway' looks like a trumpet and 'Carlton', lemon with a frilled cup, is one of the most popular cut flowers (see p. 13). 'Camelot' has a very round flower. Often regarded as the perfect large cup, 'St Keverne' is a deep clear yellow; it is resistant to basal rot and has been used successfully in breeding (see p. 6).

There are numerous yellow-petalled cultivars with orange or red cups in various shades. Most catalogues list 'Ceylon', 'Sealing Wax', 'Home Fires' and the very tall 'Red Devon', Y–R; and 'Border Legend', 'Fortune', another popular cut flower, 'Carbineer' and 'Armada', Y–O.

Some of the many different bicolours in this Division are 'Kilworth' W–R; 'Flower Record' (see p.6) and 'Sempre Avanti', W–O; 'Salome' W–PPY; and 'Polindra' W–Y. Reverse bicolours (Y–W) include 'Binkie' and 'Daydream'.

Among the good whites (W–W) are 'Easter Moon', 'Desdemona' and 'Stainless', together with show cultivars like 'Ben Hee' and 'Canisp'. 'Ice Follies' has a wide frilled cup which opens pale yellow and soon turns white.

Above: some daffodils have yellow trumpets which become pale cream or pure white with age

Below left: 'Mrs R. O. Backhouse' was raised in 1923 by its namesake, a member of a notable family of daffodil breeders, and was the first pink trumpet to win fame

Below right: 'Red Devon', introduced in 1943, is still grown on a limited scale as a market cut flower

'Verger', a most attractive small-cupped daffodil raised in Holland in 1930

DIVISION 3: SMALL-CUPPED DAFFODILS

Many of these have white petals and white or red cups and there are few all-yellows. An exception is the dwarf 'Yellow Xit' Y–Y. As in other Divisions, some cultivars are borderline, particularly those resembling the Poeticus daffodils of Division 9.

Fine examples of yellow and red flowers (Y–R) are 'Birma' (not to be confused with 'Burma', an old large cup), 'Chunking' and 'Jezebel'. Other bicolours are 'Barrett Browning', 'La Riante' and 'Verger', which is similar to a Poet, W–R; and the large 'Park Springs' and small 'Segovia', W–Y. 'Merlin' W–GYR is sumptuous but pricey.

All-white cultivars (W–W) include 'Chinese White' and 'Verona', which are reasonably priced although not widely listed. 'Frigid' W–GWW is late flowering. Several more are appearing, often at higher prices, such as 'Cool Crystal' (see p. 53) and the diminutive 'Picoblanco' and 'Xit'.

DIVISION 4: DOUBLE DAFFODILS

Some of the doubles with only one bloom tend to become top-heavy and unable to support the flowers in bad weather. However, the traditional English double daffodil, 'Van Sion' Y–Y, which has been grown for more than three centuries, seems to survive all but the worst conditions once established, especially when left untouched in a hedgerow or rough grass. It is also known as "Telamonius Plenus", "Von Sion" and, formerly, "Vincent Sion" and is extremely variable, although bulbs do not reproduce the same variations in successive seasons. Some flowers have all the double petals inside the trumpet, while others can be almost dahlia-like without any discernible trumpet. 'Camellia' and 'Inglescombe', Y–Y, are more regular in being fully double, but paler and less robust than 'Van Sion'. 'Golden Ducat' Y–Y is richly coloured and becoming a popular cut flower.

'Mary Copeland' W–O, 'Irene Copeland' W–Y and 'White Lion' W–W are three inexpensive cultivars of different colours.

'Eystettensis' Y–Y, often called "Capax Plenus" or "Queen Anne's Double Daffodil", is a survival from the distant past and almost unique in appearance, with its regular arrangement of slender uniform petals in tiers. 'Rip van Winkle' also has fully double flowers and is very distinctive with its petals like crochet hooks, while 'Pencrebar' resembles a double Jonquil. The "Double White", N. poeticus 'Flore Pleno' W–W, is sweetly scented.

At slightly higher prices are some modern cultivars like 'Acropolis' W–R, 'Double Event' and 'Unique', W–Y, 'Gay Challenger' W–O, and 'Fiji' Y–Y. Many more expensive doubles are being raised and offered.

Among the double daffodils with multiple blooms, most of which are scented, 'Cheerfulness' W–W (see p. 16) and its sport, 'Yellow Cheerfulness' Y–Y are well known. 'Erlicheer' W–W, as the name implies, is similar to 'Cheerfulness' but earlier-flowering. Others of the same type are 'Bridal Crown' W–W and 'Sir Winston Churchill' W–O. 'White Marvel' W–W is a double sport of the Triandrus 'Tresamble'.

DIVISION 5: TRIANDRUS DAFFODILS

'April Tears', 'Hawera' (see p. 44), 'Liberty Bells' and 'Thoughtful', Y–Y, together with 'Tresamble', 'Thalia', 'Niveth', 'Arish Mell' and 'Rippling Waters', W–W, are all good examples of this Division. 'Silver Chimes', originally registered here, is now included in Division 8.

DIVISION 6: CYCLAMINEUS DAFFODILS

Most of these cultivars flower early, particularly 'February Gold' Y–Y, which usually lives up to its name, and 'February Silver' W–Y, with a very pale cup, not far behind. 'Bartley' and 'Peeping Tom', Y–Y, are similar but seem to vary in growth from

Above: 'Hawera', a charming Triandrus cultivar bred in New Zealand, has attracted great attention at shows recently

Below: Cyclamineus daffodils are invaluable garden plants, many with long-lasting flowers appearing in early March

Above: a young flower of 'Waterperry', a Jonquilla daffodil, which develops a pinkish apricot cup

Below: 'Highfield Beauty', a modern Poetaz with striking flowers, usually three to a stem

garden to garden. The rich yellow 'Tête-à-Tête' Y–Y (see p. 57) has become very popular recently, although like 'Beryl' Y–O and others, some stocks are virus-infected. 'Jenny' W–Y tends to become paler as it matures (see p. 18). Also worth mentioning are the brightly coloured 'Jack Snipe' (see p. 23) and lighter 'Dove Wings', W–Y (see p. 37); 'Little Witch' and 'Garden Princess', Y–Y, both good yellow cultivars; and 'Larkelly' and 'Larkwhistle', Y–O, with their contrasting orange cups. 'Charity May' Y–Y is an unusual soft primrose yellow (see p. 6). 'Jetfire' and 'Quince', Y–O, are notable for their refined flowers, together with 'Jumblie' Y–Y.

'Foundling', the first of the pink Cyclamineus (W–P), has been followed by others like 'Lavender Lass'. As with so many Divisions, a number of new and more expensive cultivars are being introduced.

DIVISION 7: JONQUILLA DAFFODILS

Vigorous cultivars include 'Trevithian', 'Shah', 'Sweetness', with strongly scented flowers, the very old 'Buttercup', and the rich 'Golden Sceptre', Y–Y; and 'Orange Queen' Y–O. Daintier and more akin to the parents are 'Bobbysoxer', 'Sundial' (see p. 18), 'Sun Disc' and 'Tittle Tattle', Y–Y; 'Waterperry' W–P (see p. 45); and 'Lintie', 'Lanarth', 'Sweet Pepper' and 'Suzy', Y–O. Most of these Jonquils also have the rich yellow colouring of the parents but vary considerably from deep lemon to almost orange yellow. The tall 'Stratosphere' Y–Y is a good modern cultivar.

DIVISION 8: TAZETTA DAFFODILS

The Tazettas proper are the least hardy of the common narcissus and are most familiar as indoor plants grown in pots or bowls for Christmas flowering. However, they are a feature of early spring in the milder areas of Britain and, planted deeply at the foot of a south-facing wall, may succeed in other parts of the country. They are also cultivated in the Isles of Scilly for the cut-flower market, arriving from November onwards. Unfortunately, supplies of the commercially grown cultivars are not plentiful.

'Grand Soleil d'Or' is the best known, often sold as "Soleil d'Or" and also known as Sol. Even less hardy is 'Paper White' W–W (see p. 11). There are two slightly stronger named forms, 'Paper White Snowflake' and 'Paper White Grandiflora', which are very similar but distinct. Except in the favoured southwest, these are really only suitable for growing in pots and bowls indoors.

Among other Tazettas (W–Y) are 'Avalanche' and 'Grand Monarque'; 'Scilly White', which is variable but mostly with very pale cups; and 'Grand Primo Citrionière', again with at least two forms, one of which has cups of a less intense yellow.

'Matador' Y–O, a fairly recent introduction from the USA, has been used in breeding. 'Golden Dawn' Y–O, also from the USA, has the unusual attribute of producing a succession of flowers from the same bulb throughout the season. Both seem to be hardier than the older Tazettas.

This Division also includes a large group of cultivars, the Poetaz, resulting from crosses between Tazettas and Poets. These are hardier and can be grown in much colder climates, although they are more often seen in bowls indoors. 'Cragford' W–R is of moderate height and ideal for growing in pots and bowls for early flowering. Others include 'Canary Bird' Y–O, 'Chinita' Y–YYR, 'Geranium' W–O (see p. 57), 'Pride of Cornwall' W–YYR, 'Scarlet Gem' Y–R and 'St Agnes' W–R. As already mentioned, 'Silver Chimes' W–Y, although rather different with its pale yellow cup, is now classified here and not in Division 5. One of the smallest Poetaz and almost Tazetta-like in appearance is 'Minnow' W–Y. 'Martha Washington' W–O and 'Highfield Beauty' W–GOO (see p. 45) are two of the boldest, with few flowers to the stem and strong growth.

DIVISION 9: POETICUS DAFFODILS

Narcissus poeticus recurvus W–GYR, often known as the "Pheasant's Eye", is considered by many to be the finest example of a Poet. It has the distinctive scent of the Division and flowers later than almost all others, in May. Like most of its fellows, it should be planted early and left untouched for many years.

The Dutch-raised 'Actaea' W–YYR (see p. 48) is the most generally available cultivar and also well known as a cut flower. However, some of the refined older Poets can still be found. They include 'Cantabile', a successful show flower, 'Felindre', 'Sonata' and 'Milan', W–GYR; 'Hexameter' W–YR; and 'Dulcimer' W–YYR. Recent breeding has produced a number of new cultivars, but prices are high and they are only listed in catalogues of specialist growers.

DIVISION 10: SPECIES, WILD FORMS AND NATURAL HYBRIDS

In theory this Division includes all daffodils found in the wild. In practice, however, the species which have been important parents of garden daffodils are often wrongly grouped with their progeny, in catalogues and at shows. *N. poeticus recurvus* W–GYR, for instance, usually appears in Division 9 and *N.*

Above: 'Actaea', raised early this century, is still grown in commercial quantities and has proved very successful as a forced bulb; it is also good for naturalizing in the garden

Below: *Narcissus cyclamineus* is a rare native of Portugal and is very distinctive for the swept back petals and long narrow corona; it does best in a moist situation

Above; 'Cassata', one of the controversial split-corona daffodils, was registered in 1963

Below: 'Taffeta' belongs to an unusual group of daffodils bred in the 1950s, which are classified in Division 12

jonquilla Y–Y, with its forms, in Division 7. Other daffodils from the wild which are generally available are *N. triandrus albus* (*N.t. triandrus*) W–W, known as "Angel's Tears", and *N. triandrus concolor* Y–Y (often listed in Division 5) and *N. cyclamineus* Y–Y (in Division 6; see p. 48).

N. bulbocodium Y–Y, the hoop-petticoat daffodil, and its many relatives are all dwarf, 4 to 8 inches (10–12 cm) high, with large cups and small petals, and are excellent for the rock garden or for pots in the greenhouse (see p. 2). *N. bulbocodium citrinus* and *N. romieuxii*, Y–Y, and *N. cantabricus* W–W are obtainable from specialist growers. Recent advances have been made in breeding from this group.

The wild English daffodil, *N. pseudonarcissus* Y–Y (see p. 9), is ideal for naturalizing in grass in an open or slightly shaded situation. Regular grass cutting after the seed has ripened will usually lead to an increase in bulbs and flowers. Daffodils of similar habit include *N. p. gayi* W–Y, *N. p. lobularis* Y–Y, and *N. p. obvallaris* Y–Y.

The smaller *N. asturiensis* and *N. minor*, Y–Y, and their various forms are much dwarfer and more slender than *N. pseudonarcissus* and can only be appreciated where they will not be over-shadowed by taller plants.

Other daffodils from the wild are sometimes offered, although many of them need special treatment if they are to succeed. One wonders how many times such species as *N. viridiflorus*, *N. elegans* and *N. serotinus* have been collected and sold, only to disappear from cultivation.

DIVISION 11: SPLIT-CORONA DAFFODILS

There are now many cultivars in this unusual Division. Those to be found in catalogues at various prices include 'Baccarat', 'Holiday Inn' and 'Kingsize', Y–Y; 'Orangery' and 'Pick Up', W–O; 'Canasta', 'Cassata' (see p. 49) and 'Tricolet', W–Y; 'Colorange' Y–O; and 'Grapillon' W–W.

DIVISION 12: MISCELLANEOUS DAFFODILS

Very few in number, these cultivars are the result of an unusual combination of parents, which means that they cannot be classified in any of the other Divisions. Examples are 'Tarlatan', 'Muslin', 'Taffeta' (see p. 49) and 'Nylon', all pale primrose to creamy white and resembling a hoop-petticoat daffodil. There is also the interesting 'Bittern' Y–O, a cross between Cyclamineus and Tazetta cultivars.

Specialist cultivation

GROWING FOR CUTTING OR EXHIBITION

Most daffodils are undemanding and will continue to give good value for many years in the garden. However, if one is striving for perfection, whether for one's own satisfaction or for competitive showing, it will be necessary to pay them rather more attention and to grow them in a specially prepared plot. A reserve bed of this kind is also the best solution if one wants to pick flowers for the house without spoiling the display in the garden.

Deeply dug soil, well manured for a previous crop such as early potatoes or early peas and broad beans, with a low-nitrogen fertilizer worked in at 2 or 3 ounces to each square yard (60–90 g per m²) should produce first-class flowers, if healthy bulbs are planted early and kept free of weeds. The most usual planting method is to plant in rows some 18 inches (45 cm) apart as one would with potatoes. A trench is taken out to the required depth, three times the height of the bulb, and the bulbs are planted about 4 inches (10 cm) apart before being covered with soil. They should not be planted too shallowly, as this tends to encourage the development of basal rot which flourishes in warm conditions.

A fine level finish to the surface will make it easier to control weeds. Perennial weeds like docks, thistles and couch grass should, of course, have been removed before planting, but it is almost impossible to prevent the growth of annual weeds. A direct-contact weed-killer, such as paraquat with diquat, may be applied at the recommended rate to destroy new weed seedlings; this can be followed by a soil-acting herbicide, for instance, pro-pachlor, which should be applied to clean weed-free soil, to reduce or stop weed seed germination for the next few weeks. If chemical herbicides are considered unacceptable in the garden, careful hoeing over the bulbs and later between the rows should be effective in a dry autumn. However, hand weeding will also be necessary, both well before flowering and once afterwards if the bulbs are to be left for another year. After the leaves have died down and been removed, further hoeing should be carried out over the tops of the bulbs until late autumn.

Planted early, about mid-September, most good bulbs should produce fine flowers the following spring, although they usually improve even more in the second and third years. If planted late, the results may be poor at first but will again be better in the second season. Many daffodil enthusiasts like to lift the bulbs in the second summer after planting, before they become crowded and the flowers smaller. Lifting should be carried out just as the leaves have turned yellow, but before they have become brittle and breaking away from the bulb. With the leaves still attached, it is much easier to trace the bulbs and unearth them by careful forking. As the bulbs are lifted, place them in a separate tray or open mesh bag with a label for each cultivar, to prevent them getting mixed up. Then move them as soon as possible to a dry airy shed for drying. Depending on the climate and amount of moisture in the atmosphere, this will take from two days to three weeks.

Once dried, the bulbs are cleaned and prepared for replanting. When sorting them, it is always wise to keep the different batches of cultivars separate and work with one kind at a time. Tip the bulbs on to a clean bench, with their label, and first discard any that are damaged or soft. These should be burned or put in the dustbin in case they are diseased. Next, remove the dry roots and any loose skins with the remains of dead leaves clinging to the top of the bulbs. Finally, detach any offsets which are very loose, but do not attempt to cut or tear away those still encased in one or more of the skins.

For storing, the bulbs are best kept dry but not too hot. Moisture will start the roots into growth and such roots may be damaged in handling and planting, while heat may shrivel the bulbs, reducing their vigour and possibly delaying flowering next spring. Early replanting rather than good storage should be the aim. Treatment of bulbs by carefully controlled temperatures (see p. 24) is likely to be too sophisticated for the amateur grower to consider.

Some of the best rounds or tight double-nosed bulbs may be selected for growing in pots indoors or for a special position in the garden. The remainder of the full-size bulbs can be planted together as before, while the offsets or chips may be set rather closer together to grow into bulbs of flowering size after one or two years. After each two-year period, one can expect to end up with about twice as many bulbs as were originally planted and, once all the available space in the garden has been exhausted, there will be the pleasure of giving away the surplus to friends.

SHOWING

Most amateur gardeners will be content to grow 'ordinary' daffodils which are widely available from the normal sources and relatively cheap. However, some may wish to experiment with

'Cool Crystal', a small-cupped daffodil raised in 1966, has received many prizes when exhibited

the more expensive kinds obtainable only from specialist growers and breeders. If they are successful and achieve particularly fine blooms in their own gardens, they may well be tempted to compare their results with others and to enter the world of competitive showing.

The newcomer to showing should start by consulting the two main annual publications on the subject – *Daffodils*, published by the Royal Horticultural Society, and the *Journal* of the Daffodil Society. These contain helpful articles, reports on the shows and classes and lists of prizewinning cultivars. Then visit the shows, talk to the experts and examine the winning exhibits, noting the quality and presentation. Some of the points which the judges look for are: straight green stems; flowers carried horizontally (except those like the Cyclamineus and Triandrus cultivars with naturally hanging heads); clean unblemished blooms with smooth edges to the petals; of a solid white, yellow or other colour, not faded or papery in appearance; and without pollen spilling from the petals, indicating an older flower which might not last the duration of the show.

It is important to read the schedule carefully before deciding what to exhibit. Study the exact description of each class, the number of blooms or stems required, whether leaves should be added (this is usually encouraged), the policy over labelling and the times of staging. Sometimes exhibitors must take their own vases, although at larger shows these are often provided. However, moss or soft paper or similar filler will be needed for packing round the stems and leaves to keep them in position. The beginner may be surprised at how long it takes to prepare and stage even a few vases. Always allow plenty of time and remember to take a few spare blooms for each class in case of mishap.

By observation, comparison and perusal of lists, one can soon learn which are the best kinds to choose for exhibition purposes. A number of daffodil growers and breeders specialize in show or exhibition cultivars, often exclusive to the raiser, and new ones are introduced every year. For this reason, there has been no attempt to make particular recommendations here, although many of the more expensive cultivars mentioned in the previous chapter would win prizes at local shows. The reader should refer to the list of suppliers on p. 64, in order to obtain catalogues listing cultivars that compete in the best company. These bulbs are more costly than garden daffodils and depth of pocket or thickness of wallet will inevitably limit one's spending.

PROPAGATION

Most species of Narcissus can be raised from seed and should come true, although this is not always so if they are growing close to others. Many garden varieties also produce viable seed, but do not come true. It is of course from seed that new cultivars are raised, which can be an exciting hobby even for the ordinary gardener (see p. 56).

All daffodils increase by division, as we have seen, and naturally double in quantity every other year. However, two recent developments have made it possible to produce much greater numbers of bulbs relatively quickly. One, known as meristem culture or micropropagation, results in more or less virus-free bulbs, but can only be carried out by specialists with the necessary facilities. The other – or rather the two closely related methods, chipping and twin-scaling – may be practised by any gardener without great expenditure of money or time and can increase the amount of bulbs about ten times each year.

Chipping is an easy operation which consists of using a sharp knife to cut large round bulbs vertically into 8 or 16 segments, each with a piece of base plate attached. Twin-scaling is more intricate and requires further cutting of the vertical segments into sections, each made up of two pieces of scale and again retaining a portion of the base. On average, one bulb will be produced from each chip or twin scale, which means that up to 16 bulbs may be obtained from chipping and more from twin-scaling.

Beginners are advised to experiment with a few of their more plentiful or less precious bulbs. These are first lifted, dried and cleaned (as explained on p. 52) and then washed in a solution of 0.5% formaldehyde to reduce the risk of contamination by fungus diseases. Sterile conditions are essential: the work bench should also be cleaned with formalin and the knife dipped regularly into a jar of methylated spirit or other commercial alcohol.

Cut off the top of the bulb at the point where it begins to swell to its greatest diameter, but not as far down as the centre, and throw the top away. Stand the bulb on its severed top and cut it vertically in half. Then cut each half vertically into two and divide these in the same way again so that there are 8 pieces of bulb, each with a part of the base attached. (Any pieces without the base attached will have to be discarded.) If the bulb is large enough, each segment can be cut once more to produce 16 chips. Dip the knife into the spirit and wipe the surface of the bench after finishing each bulb.

To progress to twin-scaling, take a sharply pointed knife, insert the tip between each pair of scales and cut down through the base, again making sure that each twin scale has a part of the base attached. After they have been cut, the chips or twin scales are put in a plastic bag to stop them drying out. A powdered fungicide such as Benlate is added and the bag is carefully shaken until all surfaces of the segments are covered with the powder. They are then transferred to thinner polythene bags, which allows oxygen to penetrate, with equal quantities of moistened perlite or vermiculite to keep the pieces separate. The bags, suitably labelled and tied at the neck, are kept in a constant temperature of 68° to 73°F (20–22°C) for 12 weeks. The lower temperature is said to produce rather fewer bulblets, but does minimize the risk of fungus infection. Good results can be achieved by using an airing cupboard or similar place with the right degree of warmth and an even temperature.

At the end of the three-month period, often about mid-September or later, each piece should have produced one or occasionally more little bulbs or bulblets which are ready to start life in the ground. The soil should be well prepared, workable, neither too dry nor too wet, and free of clods, large stones and weeds. The bulblets are planted some 2 to 3 inches (5–8 cm) deep, with an inch or two (2–5 cm) between each, and in rows 18 inches (45 cm) apart. Shallower planting leads to thin bulbs with feeble roots weakened by the effort to pull the bulbs deeper into the soil. The best position is probably in open ground, where the bulbs can be covered by cloches from the time of planting until the following spring, although in cold districts it might be safer to plant under cover, on the greenhouse floor or in frames. They are then left for a total of some 21 months, before being lifted for replanting at a wider spacing, to grow into round bulbs which will flower three or four years after the initial cutting of the chips and twin scales.

BREEDING

Saving and sowing seed is a rewarding pastime for the gardener. It can yield considerable quantities of plants and create interest and surprise at the many variations produced. With daffodils, however, the casual picking of a few seed pods, even from the best flowers, is not very practical, The time scale is too long, involving a wait of at least four years for the first results, and the seedlings from such a haphazard collection are likely to be very mixed. Many breeders may have started in this way, but those who succeed soon have to adopt definite objectives for their breeding programme – larger or more shapely flowers, perhaps, earlier or later blooms than usual, or richer colours, particularly in the oranges and reds. It seems difficult to imagine what further improvements could be made on existing cultivars. But there is still enormous potential, especially in the use of previously untried species as parents.

The amateur interested in breeding should first decide on the sort of new flower being aimed at and then seek likely parents. There is generally a direct connection between the two parents and the progeny but, since all daffodils have such mixed forebears, unexpected seedlings always arise. In some cases, these may be equally acceptable for growing on and naming. However, to prevent unwanted outside pollination and obtain any degree of certainty that the seedlings will be from the intended parents, the flowers of both the chosen female and male plants should be protected from insects. This is done by enclosing them in a bag of paper, opaque plastic or muslin just as they are about to open. The

Above: a trial of narcissus grown at the RHS Garden, Wisley

Below left: 'Geranium', a fine old Poetaz and reliable show cultivar; it is especially good for forcing

Below right: 'Tête-à-Tête', an extremely popular Cyclamineus daffodil, equally at home in bowls indoors or outside in the garden; it is early flowering and increases freely

anthers should also be removed from the flower of the mother plant, before it has expanded naturally, in order to avoid self-pollination. A few days after the flower has fully opened on the male parent, the pollen will be ready and can be transferred direct to the stigma of the female. The pollinated flower should then be labelled with the names of the parents and the date and the protective bag replaced for a few days until fertilization is complete.

It is also possible to save pollen from early-flowering kinds for application to later flowers if such crosses are wanted. Many breeders find it more efficient to work with bulbs grown in pots, which can be stood on a bench in the greenhouse at a convenient height and can be protected more easily from chance pollination.

The seed pods should swell and turn yellow or brown as the seed within ripens, usually towards the end of June and in July. It is advisable to inspect the plants daily in order to collect each pod as it begins to split open, before the seed has been dropped and lost. The pods, with their labels, should be put into paper bags – not plastic, which could cause the seed to rot.

The seed is best sown as soon as possible, although it does no harm to save it until the last batch has been harvested and to sow all at once. Use 7-inch (18 cm) pots or larger, since these will allow room for root growth and are less likely to dry out, and one pot for each seed pod. Sow the seeds in fine seed compost about an inch (2.5 cm) apart, covering to the same depth as the thickness of the seed. They should be protected from direct sunlight after sowing and from freezing temperatures during the winter. A thin grass-like leaf can be expected from each seed the following year and in the second year usually two recognizable daffodil leaves will appear. When these have died down, the young bulbs may be shaken out of the pots and planted in rows outside, about 3 inches (8 cm) apart and 2 inches (5 cm) deep.

Some seedlings may flower after four years (two years after the first transplanting), others may take from five to seven years. At this stage, the motley crowd of seedlings with their varying leaves and mixtures of flowers can be assessed and any obviously worthless seedlings thrown out. The rest are transplanted into rows with 3 or 4 inches (8–10 cm) between the bulbs for another season or two of flowering.

The ordinary gardener who is experimenting with breeding will probably be very reluctant to discard any seedlings after waiting so long for results. For the purposes of competitive showing, however, it is necessary to be ruthless and keep only those which are of exceptional quality or outstandingly different. Similarly, the temptation to name one's best seedling should be resisted until it has flowered at least three times and proved its merits or received an award at one of the major shows. The indiscriminate naming of new cultivars, many of which subsequently disappear, has led to great confusion. As a result, all daffodil names are now registered with the Royal Horticultural Society, as the International Registration Authority for *Narcissus* cultivar names. Any proposed new name should be submitted to the Society for registration and, if the application is accepted, will then appear in a supplement to the *International Narcissus Register.*

DISEASES, DISORDERS AND PESTS

Almost all garden plants suffer attack from various pests and diseases and the daffodil is no exception. However, compared to many other ornamentals, daffodils are relatively trouble-free. The average gardener has little to worry about and would be well advised to accept a few failures or losses rather than resort to sprays, dusts and other treatments.

The daffodil enthusiast, on the other hand, who is intent on growing top-quality flowers, exhibiting, or breeding new cultivars, will need to know more about the enemies which might be encountered and how to combat them. The following notes, therefore, are chiefly for the benefit of the specialist and are not intended to alarm the amateur. Additional information has been kindly provided by Miss A. V. Brooks and Mr Andrew Halstead, plant pathologist and entomologist at the RHS Garden, Wisley.

Fungus diseases

Narcissus basal rot has become particularly virulent in recent years and does more damage in warm wet conditions. It is often first noticed on stored bulbs, when the disease starts at the basal plate of the bulb, which becomes soft, and then moves upwards, causing a chocolate brown discolouration of the inner scales and pink fungal growth. The many spores produced spread the disease to other bulbs in store. Bulbs can also be affected during the growing season, as the fungus is soil-borne. Severe infection will result in yellowing of the leaf tips or complete death of the leaves and in wet periods in heavy soil the disease may kill the bulbs underground so that no foliage emerges. Over several seasons plants will disappear from a progessively large area. In less serious attacks the disease may not be detected until lifting, when the bulbs will look soft and decayed, or until the bulbs rot in store.

All affected bulbs, including those that feel soft, should be destroyed. The remainder should be dipped after lifting as a precaution (see below). Replant only firm healthy bulbs in the autumn planting them more deeply than usual in very well drained soil and on a different site.

Narcissus leaf or tip scorch survives in the dry papery scales of the bulb and does not usually rot the bulb itself. The fungus attacks the leaves as they emerge from the bulb, giving them a scorched or burnt appearance at the tips and sometimes making them stick together. The buds and flowers are often attacked in damp weather and should be removed as soon as they die.

Remove and burn affected leaf tips. Spray with benomyl, carbendazim, thiophanate-methyl or mancozeb when the foliage is about 3 inches (8 cm) high, repeating two or three times before flowering and once afterwards if necessary. The disease is also controlled by dipping (see below).

Narcissus smoulder is most prevalent in cold wet seasons and is recognizable as spotting or even rotting of the foliage and flowers. It also leads to the decay of bulbs in store. The fungus persists from one year to another in the form of small black resting bodies (sclerotia), which are present in the soil and also in and on the outer bulb scales. Infected bulbs produce distorted yellow shoots with withered dark brown or black leaf tips. In warm dry weather the affected tissues dry up and the plants flower normally, but in wet weather the diseased leaves stick together and become covered with grey masses of spores. These can be spread by wind or rain splash to infect other leaves and flowers, resulting in spotting or further rotting.

Any decaying bulbs or those bearing large numbers of sclerotia should be destroyed. Plants showing symptoms should be sprayed as for leaf scorch. Dipping (see below) will also give protection.

Dipping of bulbs after lifting is a good preventive measure against fungus diseases. The bulbs are lifted as soon as possible after the foliage has died down and carefully examined. Any which show signs of rotting, however slight, or softness, or have significant numbers of the black resting bodies of fungi should be destroyed.

Within 48 hours of lifting, dip the bulbs for at least 30 minutes in a suspension of benomyl or carbendazim or thiophanate-methyl. This should be made up at the rate of $1\frac{1}{2}$ ounces in 5 gallons (42 g in 22 litres) of water, in the absence of manufacturer's instructions for dipping. Tepid water is preferable and the suspension should be kept agitated throughout. The bulbs should then be dried off rapidly before storing in well ventilated, cool, but frost-proof conditions. Check through the bulbs at intervals and remove any decaying bulbs. Replanting should be done on a fresh site when soil-borne diseases are known to be present.

During the following growing season the plants should not be sprayed with benomyl, carbendazim or thiophanate-methyl if one of these fungicides was previously used as a dip.

Virus diseases

Of the 18 viruses reported to afflict narcissus, not all are exclusive to daffodils and only 11 have been detected in stocks of trumpet daffodils in England and two in N. tazetta. Some of these viruses are borne by aphids, others are transmitted by eelworms in the soil. The symptoms vary greatly, depending on which virus or viruses are present and also on the cultivar concerned. In mild attacks faint mottling of the foliage may occur, particularly at the base of the leaves. In severe cases yellowish spots and streaks develop along the leaves, being most apparent in February and March. The flowers may show slight white streaks or flecks, but diseased plants eventually fail to flower and become stunted.

There is no cure and the only solution is to dig out and burn or destroy all affected bulbs.

Disorders

Daffodils which produce fewer flowers and increasing numbers of thin leaves as the years go by may be affected by a virus disease (see above), in which case they should all be thrown out. However, the condition is much more likely to be the result of overcrowding and may be dealt with as explained on p. 28.

Pests

Slugs and snails are common pests and, although they generally ignore the leaves, they can cause extensive damage to the flowers when these are bowed over in wet weather. Their numbers can be reduced by scattering slug pellets among the plants or by spraying with liquid slug killer and it is worth shaking the flowers carefully so that they stand up out of reach of the attackers.

Narcissus eelworm is a microscopic nematode almost invisible to the naked eye. It lives within the bulbs and foliage and is the most destructive pest of garden daffodils. It causes stunted, distorted growth and the leaves may develop small yellowish-brown rough patches called spickels. An infested bulb cut transversely in half will show several concentric brown rings where the eelworms have been feeding. The bulbs eventually die and, as the nematodes move through the soil to find new host plants, the area of contaminated land gradually increases.

None of the chemicals available to amateur gardeners controls narcissus eelworm. Once its presence in a garden has been diagnosed, great care should be taken to restrict its spread and to avoid moving plants or infested soil. Affected bulbs and any other host plants within a radius of one yard (0.9 m) should be removed and burnt. Daffodils and other susceptible plants, such as bluebells, snowdrops, primroses, onions, peas, beans and strawberries, should not be planted in contaminated ground for a minimum of two years. Weeds, some of which are host plants, should also be kept at bay.

It is possible to control narcissus eelworm in lightly infested bulbs by hot water treatment. After lifting, bulbs are immersed for three hours in water maintained at a temperature of 112°F (44.4°C). The temperature is critical and must be precisely controlled if the pest is to be killed without harming the bulbs. (Further details of this technique, which also controls narcissus fly and bulb scale mite, are given in MAFF Reference Book 201, 'Hot-Water Treatment of Plant Material', published by HMSO, 1986.)

The large narcissus fly resembles a small humble-bee and is about ½ inch (1.2 cm) long, with black, yellow or ginger hairs. The adults are active on sunny days in late April to June, when the females lay single eggs in the neck of narcissus bulbs. After hatching, the maggot, normally only one per bulb, crawls down the outside of the bulb and enters through the basal plate. It feeds on the centre of the bulb, filling it with mud-like droppings, and the following spring goes into the soil to pupate. Damaged bulbs are often killed and at best produce only a few thin grass-like leaves.

In most gardens losses caused by this pest are not too serious. However, in warm sheltered places, where the adult flies flourish, daffodils will be more vulnerable. For similar reasons, bulbs should not be left in the sunshine to dry off after lifting. Large narcissus fly is difficult to control with insecticides, but some protection can be given to valuable bulbs by dusting the neck region with HCH to deter the females from laying eggs. Great satisfaction can also be had with a butterfly net. It helps too if soil is drawn up around the neck of the bulbs as the foliage starts to die down.

Small narcissus fly is not an important pest, since the adults lay eggs in bulbs already damaged by some other pest, disease or physical injury, unlike the large narcissus fly which attacks sound bulbs. If several small maggots up to $\frac{1}{4}$ inch (0.6 cm) long are found inside a decaying bulb, they are likely to be larvae of the small narcissus fly and it then becomes necessary to identify and treat the primary cause of the problem.

Bulb scale mite normally attacks indoor bulbs forced for early flowering, although it occasionally occurs in outdoor bulbs. The microscopic mites live in the neck of the bulb, where they feed on the developing leaves and flowers. This causes the foliage to be sickle-shaped and the flower stems misshapen and stunted. The edges of both flowers stems and leaves have distinctive sawtooth scars.

None of the chemicals available to amateur gardeners controls this mite and affected plants should be destroyed. The most sensible precaution is to buy bulbs for forcing from reputable suppliers.

Daffodils look best grown in a mass

Suppliers

Avon Bulbs – general: dwarf daffodils and garden cultivars
Bradford-on-Avon, Wilts, BA15 2AT

Mrs J. Abel Smith – specialist: exhibition cultivars, mostly own varieties
Orchard House, Letty Green, Hertford, Herts. SG14 2NZ

Jacques Amand Ltd – general: popular garden cultivars
17 Beethoven Street, London W10 4LG

Ballydorn Bulb Farm – specialist: show cultivars mainly of own raising
Killinchy, Newtownards, Co. Down BT23 6QB

Walter Blom & Son Ltd – general: garden cultivars
Leavesden, Watford, Herts. WD2 7BH

Broadleigh Gardens – general: wide range of dwarf daffodils and good
garden cultivars, especially Divisions 5, 6, and 7
Bishops Hull, Taunton, Somerset TA4 1AE

Carncairn Daffodils Ltd – specialist: many of their own exhibition
cultivars and some older cheaper varieties
Carncairn Lodge, Broughshane, Co. Antrim BT43 7HF

P. de Jager & Sons Ltd/Wallace & Barr Ltd – general: garden cultivars
The Nurseries, Marden, Kent TN12 9BP

Michael Jefferson-Brown Ltd – specialist: a few expensive show cultivars
and some good garden daffodils both unusual and common
Broadgate, Weston Hills, Spalding, Lincs. PE12 6DQ

Kelways Nurseries – general: popular garden cultivars
Langport, Somerset TA10 9SL

J. Parker – general: popular garden cultivars
452 Chester Road, Old Trafford, Manchester M16 9HL

Clive Postles Daffodils – specialist: exhibition cultivars
The Old Cottage, Purshull Green, Droitwich, Worcs. WR9 0NL

Rathowen Daffodils – specialist: show cultivars, many of own raising
Knowehead, Dergmoney, Omagh, Co. Tyrone BT78 1PN

Tamar Valley Daffodils – specialist: a few exhibition cultivars, plus good
value old varieties and garden daffodils
du Plessis Brothers, Marsh Farm, Landulph, Saltash, Cornwall PL12
6NG

Van Tubergen – general: well known garden cultivars and some species
Oldfield Lane, Wisbech, Cambs. PE13 2RJ

R. W. Ward – specialist: wide range including Tazettas and split-corona
daffodils
Normandy, St Mary's, Isles of Scilly TR21 0NY